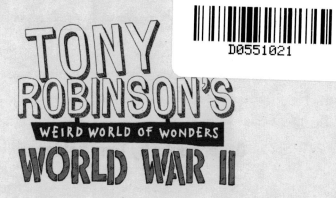

# TONY ROBINSON'S
### WEIRD WORLD OF WONDERS
# WORLD WAR II

**Tony Robinson** has been scribbling away since he was old enough to pick up a pencil. He's written long stuff (last year he wrote a history of Australia), and shorter stuff (like this). He's rewritten old stories (like the ones about the Greek heroes Odysseus and Theseus), and made up new ones (for instance his children's TV series *Tales from Fat Tulip's Garden*). But history is what he likes best, because he says, 'How do you know who you are if you don't know where you came from?' That's why he's written Tony Robinson's Weird World of Wonders, and he doesn't want to stop until he's written about every single bit of history there's ever been - although in order to do this he'll have to live till he's 8,374!

**Del Thorpe** has been drawing ever since that time he ruined his mum's best tablecloth with wax crayons. Most of his formative work can be found in the margins of his old school exercise books. His maths teacher described these misunderstood works as 'wasting time'. When he left normal school, Del went to art school and drew serious, grown-up things. Soon he decided the grown-up stuff was mostly boring, so went back to drawing silly cartoons and has done ever since.

## Other books by Tony Robinson

The Worst Children's Jobs in History

Bad Kids

Tony Robinson's Weird World of Wonders: Romans

Tony Robinson's Weird World of Wonders: Egyptians

Tony Robinson's Weird World of Wonders: Greeks

Tony Robinson's Weird World of Wonders: British

Tony Robinson's Weird World of Wonders: Funny Inventions

# TONY ROBINSON'S

## WEIRD WORLD OF WONDERS

# WORLD WAR II

Illustrated by
Del Thorpe

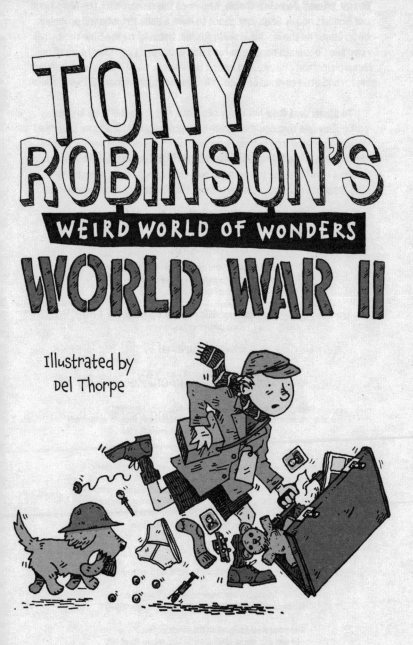

MACMILLAN CHILDREN'S BOOKS

**To my friend Jessica Cobb**, who does the research for the Weird World of Wonders books. She's just about to have a baby girl, who will probably be as clever as she is. This is great for me, because by the time the baby's two she's bound to be able to read and write, and I'll get her to do all my research instead of Jess; and I won't have to pay her, I'll just give her penny sweets and little cartons of juice. It'll save me loads of money! Thanks, Jess.

**To Mum and Dad** Not many of us know what it's like to be in a war, particularly one that could end with our country being taken over by a cruel and racist dictator. But my mum and dad's generation spent six years of their lives in the fight against Hitler, and if it wasn't for them Britain would be a horrible place to live in. We owe them a huge debt of gratitude. So thanks Mum, thanks Dad, and sorry I was a little monster sometimes.

First published 2013 by Macmillan Children's Books

This edition published 2013 by Macmillan Children's Books
a division of Macmillan Publishers Limited
20 New Wharf Road, London N1 9RR
Basingstoke and Oxford
Associated companies throughout the world
www.panmacmillan.com

ISBN 978-1-4472-5141-5

Text copyright © Tony Robinson 2013
Illustrations copyright © Del Thorpe 2013

The right of Tony Robinson and Del Thorpe to be identified as the
author and illustrator of this work has been asserted by them in accordance
with the Copyright, Designs and Patents Act 1988.

All rights reserved. No part of this publication may be
reproduced, stored in or introduced into a retrieval system, or
transmitted, in any form or by any means (electronic, mechanical,
photocopying, recording or otherwise), without the prior written
permission of the publisher. Any person who does any unauthorized
act in relation to this publication may be liable to criminal
prosecution and civil claims for damages.

1 3 5 7 9 8 6 4 2

A CIP catalogue record for this book is available from the British Library.

Typeset by Dan Newman/Perfect Bound Ltd
Printed and bound by CPI Group (UK) Ltd, Croydon CR0 4YY

This book is sold subject to the condition that it shall not,
by way of trade or otherwise, be lent, resold, hired out,
or otherwise circulated without the publisher's prior consent
in any form of binding or cover other than that in which
it is published and without a similar condition including this
condition being imposed on the subsequent purchaser.

**Hello, we're the Curiosity Crew. You'll probably spot us hanging about in this book checking stuff out.**

It's about wheelbarrows full of money and things that go bang.
It's about friends and enemies, and standing up to bullies.
It's also about moustaches, secret codes and
plenty more besides!

Read on to find out ...

# INTRODUCTION

BOOM!

In 1914 the biggest war ever broke out across the world – millions of people were killed or injured.

BOOM!

It was a war so big it was called **'The Great War'.**

. . . And it dragged on for four muddy, bloody and brutal years. When it finally ended everyone breathed a huge sigh of relief, safe in the knowledge that nothing so horrible would be allowed to happen ever again.

Phew!!!

3

Everyone went back to their everyday lives.

Films, which until then had been silent and in black-and-white, now had sound and colour!

Girls cut their hair into bobs, wore short flappy dresses, and did a crazy dance called the Charleston.

People drove cars and travelled by plane, and visited places they'd never been to before.

Inventors came up with thousands of crazy inventions like the ballpoint pen and the chocolate chip cookie.

Jazz records sold by the thousand and went to the top of the charts.

Then suddenly ... *EVERYBODY DUCK!*

... this happened.

Germany invaded Poland.

It happened at 4.40 a.m. on 1 September 1939 while most people were still tucked up in bed asleep. Planes appeared overhead and started dropping bombs. (The Poles soon woke up – there's nothing like earth-shattering explosions to get you going in the morning.) More than a million German soldiers flooded across the Polish border, armed with a frightening array of state-of-the-art weapons and supported by tanks and aircraft. The Germans called this attack . . .

Nobody had ever seen anything like it!

Blitzkrieg means 'lightning war'.

They moved lightning-fast, capturing towns and cities, executing anyone who stood in their way. Wave after wave of planes destroyed railways and roads, and gunned down people who tried to run off. There was total chaos.

'Oi,' said Britain and France, 'this is no way to behave! Back off!' And they declared war on Germany.

World War Two had begun, and it would turn out to be even bigger and deadlier than the Great War.

In fact it was the biggest and deadliest war in history!

That's really something because there'd been loads of wars before.

Yeah, between Stone Age tribes, between ancient empires, between great kingdoms . . .

Some, like the Hundred Years War, went on for ages.

One, called the Anglo-Zanzibar war, only lasted 38 minutes!

World War Two involved 61 countries and more than 100 million fighting men! It went on for six years and by the time it was over a colossal 70 million people had died.

So what was it all about? Why did Germany invade Poland, and what happened next?

# CHAPTER ONE
# THE WEIRDO WITH A GLEAM IN HIS EYES

So what made the Germans start World War Two? It's not like they just woke up one morning and said to one another, 'Hey, I've got a really crazy idea. Let's invade Poland!'

Guess which one of these blokes will soon become a megalomaniac dictator?

## HITLER THE CRY BABY

Among the thousands of German men who had fought in World War One was a weirdly weird weirdo with a crazy gleam in his eyes. His name was Adolf Hitler.

He loved being a soldier. He used to volunteer for all the mad, dangerous jobs like running between the trenches with messages while dodging falling bombs. Several times he narrowly escaped being blown to bits.

He won lots of medals for bravery, but his fellow soldiers, who were fed up with the rotten food, the muddy trenches and being shot at every day, thought he was a nutter. They fancied going home, but Adolf told them that anyone who wanted to bottle out was a traitor.

When his beloved Germany finally surrendered, Hitler was gutted. In fact he was so upset he cried for days.

It had all started twenty years earlier at the end of the Great War. The Germans had lost, and they weren't at all happy about it. The trouble was that the countries which won (like America, Britain and France) wanted them to pay for all the damage that had been done (which was A LOT – the total bill came to £22,000,000,000. War isn't cheap!).

The Germans were bewildered and angry. They had thought they were going to win. They HAD been winning in the beginning. And now they were supposed to pay back all this money. How unfair can you get!

# THE WHOLE WORLD GETS DEPRESSED

While the Germans were moaning about how badly they were being treated, everyone else was busy celebrating the end of the war, spending money on jazz records, cars, and chocolate chip cookies.

Unemployed people queueing for food

This dreadful time was called the 'Great Depression'.

That was a good name for it!

But then suddenly in 1929 the whole world went bust! Banks and businesses closed, people lost their jobs because there was no money to pay their wages, and families couldn't afford food or heating.

Life may have been bad everywhere else, but in Germany, they had to pay off their colossal debt too. For ordinary Germans things were truly desperate!

## MONEY IN A WHEELBARROW

Imagine if you had a machine that could print money – just think of all the things you could buy!

1,642 pairs of trainers!

The entire Manchester United First Team . . . plus the reserves!

A bone the size of the Isle of Wight!

But believe it or not, it's possible to have too much of the stuff. In Germany in the early 1920s, the government printed more and more paper notes to try and make up for the lack of money.

Soon there were banknotes everywhere! So many were printed that they became almost worthless. You had to fill a wheelbarrow with banknotes to buy a loaf of bread!

Sometimes a robber would nick the wheelbarrow and leave the money on the ground because it wasn't worth anything. Lots of people gave the contents of their wallets to their children to play with, or made kites out of all the different-coloured notes!

What could the Germans do to get out of this mess? They didn't have anything to eat and the future looked grim.

The politicians weren't any help. They just argued with each other all the time. People thought they needed somebody to sort things out for them – someone who could make Germany rich and successful again . . .

The German Emperor and Hitler

# NASTY NAZIS

By now Hitler was the leader of a bunch of people called the 'Nationalist Socialist German Workers Party' (or 'Nazis' for short) who were all very upset about losing the war. Hitler said Germany would have won if CERTAIN PEOPLE hadn't sabotaged the war effort. And if Germany hadn't lost the war, the German people wouldn't have owed 22 billion pounds. And if they didn't owe 22 billion pounds they'd be rich and happy. And who do you think the CERTAIN PEOPLE were that Hitler was on about?

**The Army Generals** . . . for coming up with terrible battle plans and sending soldiers to their deaths?

**The Politicians** . . . for starting the war in the first place but not giving the soldiers enough weapons?

**The German soldiers** . . . for losing the will to fight and not being able to beat the enemy?

**The Jews** . . . for, um . . .being Jewish?

The answer is – he blamed them all . . . but particularly the Jews!

Let's face it – he was stupid and crazy!

# I BLAME THE JEWS BECAUSE I'M DUMB

The Jewish religion has been around for thousands of years; it's even older than other big religions like Christianity and Islam.

Lots of Jews have special customs like going to synagogue (a place of worship), wearing symbolic clothing (like a little cap called a 'Kippah'), living together in one community, and speaking a special language called Hebrew.

All in all, pretty harmless stuff. Yet throughout history Jewish people have been blamed when things go wrong.

Why?

It's probably because people can be stupid and often like blaming other folk for their problems, and as Jews are often seen as 'different', they're an easy target.

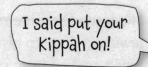

I said put your Kippah on!

Hitler at a Nazi rally

Hitler made rabble-rousing speeches about what the Jews had done to his beloved country. He ranted and raved, rocked from side to side, his eyes bulging, his hands waving, his voice getting louder and louder, and with sweat pouring off him.

He was as mad as a box of frogs but he was very good at making speeches, and people grew to believe he could make Germany great again. By 1933 the Nazi Party had 800,000 members, and Hitler was so popular he was made the ruler of Germany!

## GOOD LUCK, BAD LUCK

Before Hitler came to power, the 'swastika' was a friendly little symbol which meant 'good luck'. But he turned it into something evil. If you wore it, it meant you were a Nazi. Most grown-ups still get upset by it.

# HEIL HITLER!

The Nazi Party became Hitler's own army. Its members wore special military-style uniforms, and had badges with special crosses on them called 'swastikas'.

Nazis marched about swinging their arms and legs (this was called 'goose-stepping'), and used a special salute, shooting their right arm straight up in the air and shouting 'Heil Hitler!'

Mum, I don't want to do that. It's stupid.

A Jewish shop, smashed by the Nazis

It looked pretty daft but you didn't want to laugh at the Nazis (at least not to their faces), because if you did, they'd beat you up. They thumped anyone they didn't like. After Hitler became leader, they marched through the cities of Germany beating up Jews and setting fire to their synagogues.

Mind you, they did stop goose-stepping after a while, because they couldn't do it properly!

I can, and it still looks stupid!

## THINGS JEWISH PEOPLE WERE NOT ALLOWED TO DO IN NAZI GERMANY

As soon as they came to power, the Nazis started introducing lots of laws that banned Jewish people from doing certain things, like:

- Marrying anyone who wasn't Jewish
- Teaching
- Working for the government
- Being a lawyer or a doctor
- Playing in public parks
- Travelling on buses and trains
- Driving
- Renting a house
- Going to school
- Owning a business
- Swimming in public swimming pools
- Being German!

## THINGS THAT JEWISH PEOPLE WERE ALLOWED TO DO IN NAZI GERMANY

Ermmm . . .

- . . . Just about nothing!

Across Germany, people started believing all this anti-Jewish nonsense. They refused to talk to their Jewish neighbours, stopped buying food from shops owned by Jews, fired their Jewish employees, and told their kids they weren't allowed to be friends with Jewish kids.

By 1933, if you were a Jew in Germany you thought seriously about moving somewhere like America or Switzerland . . . in fact anywhere that wasn't Germany. Thousands packed their bags and left home to find a new life. But not everyone could afford to leave. For those who stayed, life got worse and worse.

Jews had to wear a star on their clothes – even when they were doing PE

# SPREADING THE HATE

It wasn't just Jews who suffered. Hitler hated gypsies, foreigners, gay and black people; he called them 'sub-human'. He made this word up because he wanted Germans to believe they weren't proper people.

# TEENAGE NAZIS

Even kids were allowed to be Nazis. Hitler created a special club called the 'Hitler Youth' for young people between the ages of ten and eighteen. He was a loony but he wasn't stupid. He knew that lots of kids believe in daft things, and that if they joined his 'club' it would be easy to brainwash them into believing anything he said. Then, when they grew up, they'd be Nazis too.

He could also use them as little spies. They were ordered to keep an eye on their parents and report them to the Nazis if they did anything suspicious. One boy called Walter Hess told them that his dad had said Hitler was a crazed lunatic. The Nazis promptly came round, marched his dad away and locked him up!

In the Hitler Youth, boys were taught how to be soldiers. They practised marching, shooting, trench digging and throwing grenades. It was all part of Hitler's big plan.

Girls were taught cooking, cleaning and bed-making. There was also the odd bit of pistol-shooting thrown in . . . because if there was ever another war, it would be useful if girls could shoot!

And don't think you could make excuses to get out of the Hitler Youth like 'I can't do marching, I've got a verruca!' A law was passed saying every kid had to join (unless they were Jewish, obviously!).

# HITLER'S CRAZY PLAN

Hitler's plan was to turn the Germans into a super-race of blond-haired, blue-eyed, muscle-bound warriors.

He wanted them to take over the whole world, so he could rule it with an iron fist.

To do that, he decided to wipe out the weak, the dirty, the old, the sick and anyone who stood in his way.

Of course, he couldn't just come out and say this, because other countries might try to stop him. He had to move quietly and step-by-step.

**1** The first step was to take control of Germany.

**2** The second was to get rid of anyone who was 'different', like Jews, and gypsies, or the old and sick. Nazi doctors started quietly killing off people with disabilities.

**3** The third step was to invade the next-door countries, get rid of the people who lived there, and replace them with superman-type Germans . . .

In 1938 his troops marched into neighbouring Austria and took it over. This made Britain and France very uneasy, but Austria didn't seemed to mind much, and nobody wanted another big war, so they kept quiet ...

Then Hitler demanded to be given part of a country called Czechoslovakia. This time there was a bit more muttering from the French and British. They really didn't like the way things were going at all.

Hitler promised that there was nothing to worry about – he said that once he'd taken a teensy bit of Czechoslovakia he'd be happy and wouldn't invade anywhere else. And almost everybody believed him!

Then he invaded the rest of Czechoslovakia. Now Britain and France felt really stupid.

Finally, in September 1939, Hitler ordered the invasion of Poland.

At last Britain and France had had enough. This meant

WAR!

# CHAPTER TWO
# THE CHARGING RHINO

**W**ithin days, more than 150,000 British soldiers had been sent across the Channel and into France – the British and French armies were going to sort Hitler out. With any luck, they'd be back in time for tea . . .

Unfortunately, stopping Hitler was easier said than done. It was like trying to step in front of a charging rhino. Four weeks after his army invaded Poland, the entire country was under German and Russian control.

Then, before the British and French armies could stop them, the Germans had torn through Belgium . . .

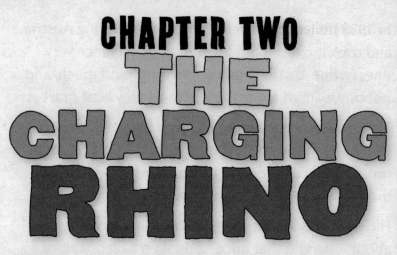

... and Holland ...

... and into northern France.

Once again German planes bombed everything and everybody, while tanks and soldiers poured across the borders and took control of France's towns and cities.

Under this terrifying pressure the French army collapsed, and the Brits retreated in order to avoid being wiped out, leaving most of their weapons and kit behind!

# THE GREAT ESCAPE

By the end of May 1940, hundreds of thousands of British and French soldiers were trapped on the French coast in a seaside resort called Dunkirk. The German forces were all around them; German bombs rained down on them, and all the Brits could do was sit on the beach and hope they'd be rescued.

The British government had a big problem. It only had enough boats to rescue about 30,000 men, and there were more than ten times that many on the beaches! What could be done?

A call for help was broadcast on the radio – 'Please will everyone who has a boat, even a small one, lend it to us so we can rescue our lads.' People responded in their hundreds. Fleets of little rowing boats, fishing boats, sailing yachts and bath tubs (well, maybe not) bobbed across the English Channel to pick up the soldiers on the French beaches.

More than 338,000 men were rescued and brought safely back to Britain. It may have been a defeat, but it felt like a victory!

British soldiers queue up to be rescued from Dunkirk

## HURRICANE HEINZ!

The German tanks were called 'Panzers', which means 'armour'.

In Germany a rhinoceros like me is called a Panzernashorn!

In the UK a rhinoceros like you is called a Big Twit!

They made a terrifying noise. Their guns boomed, their engines roared, their tank tracks clanked and clattered. It was impossible to tell when the enemy was firing because the tanks always made such an ear-splitting din!

The man in charge of the Panzers was Heinz Guderian, but because his tanks moved so fast, flattening everything that stood in their way, he was known as 'Hurricane Heinz'.

# THE BATTLE FOR BRITAIN

The Germans were over the moon. They'd already beaten Poland, Holland, Belgium, Denmark, Norway and France. It was like they were playing football and were 10-nil up after twenty minutes. Now was the time to prepare for the invasion of Britain.

Hitler decided to land 160,000 men in boats along the coast of England. The German soldiers assembled and waited for their instructions. It looked like the British were about to be on the receiving end of a terrible thrashing. Some people thought they should give up right away and start practising the goose-step. Those people had never met Winston Churchill.

We shall fight on the beaches, we shall fight on the landing grounds, we shall fight in the fields and in the streets, we shall fight in the hills; we shall never surrender!

Hitler wasn't the only leader with the gift of the gab. Winston Churchill was the Prime Minister of Britain, and he wowed the British people with his speeches. He was a large, funny-looking man who wore a bowler hat and smoked a big cigar. The Russians called him the 'British Bulldog' because he was so strong and stubborn.

Churchill thought Britain and its Empire were the best things since sliced bread and chocolate spread, and he had no intention of letting Hitler and his army stomp all over them. He'd always enjoyed a good battle. When he was a boy, he used to spend hours playing with thousands of toy soldiers on his nursery floor.

Later when he grew up he joined the army. He was shot at in Cuba, rode a horse in India, fought in the Sudan and was captured and escaped in South Africa. In World War One he was put in charge of the British Navy, and later led a battalion of soldiers on the Western Front. If Hitler wanted a fight, the 'British Bulldog' knew how to give him one.

Have you seen a bull? You wouldn't mess with a dog that could win a fight with one of those fierce things, would you?

Before Hitler could launch his invasion, he needed to be able to control the skies, otherwise British planes would bomb his ships as they sailed across the sea towards the south coast of Britain. So he ordered the German Air Force to attack and destroy all the RAF's planes and blow up its aerodromes and runways. But Churchill was determined that this wouldn't happen.

For the next two months German and British planes fought each other for control of the skies. This huge air battle became known as 'The Battle of Britain'.

# AIR WARS

Planes were a pretty new idea. A few had been used in World War One, but back then they'd been made of bits of fabric and wood held together with glue. They were so rickety that sometimes they fell apart in mid-flight. But by 1939 Britain's planes had been given a serious upgrade. They were now made out of metal, were faster and stronger, and had gadgets like radios and heavy machine guns.

Both sides had two main types of plane:

'**Bombers**' (like the British 'Wellington' and the German 'Heinkel 177'), which were big and slow and were built to carry and drop bombs . . .

and '**Fighters**' (like the German 'Messerschmitt 109' and the British 'Spitfire' and 'Hurricane'), which were small and zippy.

Being a pilot in World War Two was no picnic – imagine climbing into a small metal box, which then shoots up thousands of metres into the air. You travel at more than 300 mph, the noise is deafening, and in front of you are a million dials and switches which never stop rattling, and which you have to watch really carefully to make sure your box doesn't fall out of the sky.

Then the real fun begins – people start to fire guns and cannons at you. You duck and dodge, and try to fire back at them. If you get hit, you have to get out of your box quick, before it hits the ground or explodes in a massive ball of flame.

"NEVER WAS SO MUCH OWED BY SO MANY TO SO FEW" THE PRIME MINISTER

## HEROES OR ZEROS?

Fighter pilots who shot down more than five enemy planes were known as 'Aces' (or 'Experten' in Germany) and became heroes back home. Some got a bit carried away and said they'd shot down more planes than they really had. By the end of the war, Luftwaffe pilots claimed to have destroyed 3,058 British planes. But that can't have been true because the RAF never had that many!

## A SAD STORY

Flight Lieutenant James Nicholson
was a British fighter pilot. In August 1940 he fought a duel with
a German Messerschmitt. He was shot in the head, half blinded,
and his Hurricane caught fire. Just as he was about to jump out,
another enemy plane flew past him, so he stayed in his burning
plane, flew after it and shot it down. Only then did he bale out,
but as his parachute drifted to earth, yet another German plane
flew by and he had to pretend to be dead so it wouldn't machine-
gun him. To make things worse, before he landed, he was fired
on by the British, who thought he was a German.

Later he was given the 'Victoria Cross', the highest award for
bravery in battle. Sadly, he died shortly before the end of the war
after his plane crashed in the Bay of Bengal.

If you jump out you'll be left thousands of metres up,
plummeting towards the earth with the wind whistling
past your ears, wondering why you ever got into the
stupid box in the first place. Then, if your parachute
opens and you land without breaking both your legs,
you'll get to do the whole thing in another box the next
day. Lucky you!

# THE DEATH RAY THAT NEVER WAS

One thing that really helped the RAF was a brilliant new invention. Before the war, rumours went round that the Nazis had created a 'Death Ray' which used invisible radio waves to bring down planes! This sent the British government into a panic, and a science boffin called Robert Watson-Watt was asked to make a British Death Ray.

After lots of experimenting, he decided it was impossible (it later turned out the Germans never made one either), but instead he came up with something else: a plane-detection system that used radio waves to spot planes coming even if they were a couple of hundred miles away.

> Did he call it 'The Watson-Watt Plane-Detection System'?

> Or 'The Magic Eye'?

It may not have been a 'Death Ray' but it was a brilliant invention.

Or 'The-Machine-For-Spotting-Enemy-Planes-From-A-Long-Way-Away'?

No, he called it 'radar' . . .

Even I knew that!

# DON'T PANIC!

While the Royal Air Force was fighting the Luftwaffe in the skies, the rest of Britain was preparing for a possible invasion from the sea.

The last time we'd been successfully invaded had been by William the Conqueror in 1066. This time we'd be ready!

All round the British coast, beaches were planted with mines and covered in tangled twists of barbed wire. Miles of steel scaffolding were erected in the shallow water, and giant blocks of concrete were scattered hither and thither to get in the way of any German landing craft or tanks.

Thousands of small concrete forts called 'pillboxes' (because their shape was a bit like a giant box for pills) were put up to guard beaches, roads and rivers; and to prevent the enemy spotting them from the air and bombing them, they were sometimes disguised to look like ice-cream kiosks, haystacks and bus shelters!

Any big open spaces were covered with old cars, buses and iron bedsteads so enemy gliders couldn't land on them. Road signs were taken down, station names were painted out and petrol pumps destroyed, all in the hope that the Nazis would get lost and run out of fuel!

And people were given posters and booklets telling them what to do if there was an invasion – with helpful advice like 'Don't Panic'.

# GOLF CLUBS TO THE RESCUE

To help defend the country, the government asked for part-time volunteers. One and a half million men signed up! They became known as the 'Home Guard'. At first they didn't have uniforms, and because they had so few weapons, they armed themselves with shotguns, truncheons, pickaxes, pitchforks and even golf clubs. Some members of the Home Guard even broke into museums and nicked the weapons on display! Others simply made their own. For example:

☐ **The DIY pike** – a knife welded on to the end of a piece of gas pipe.

☐ **The DIY grenade** (or 'Molotov Cocktail') – a glass bottle filled with petrol, with a bit of cloth stuck in the neck. The cloth was set alight and someone threw the bottle. When it hit its target, the bottle smashed and blazing petrol went everywhere.

☐ **The DIY bomber** – a sparrow carrying a box of fireworks and a book of matches.

Actually this one isn't true!

Another common Home Guard weapon was the '**sticky bomb**', which was a glass globe wrapped in a glue-like covering containing high explosive. When it was thrown, it 'stuck' to its target and then exploded. The problem was that if you weren't very good at throwing, it stuck to other things – like your clothes! Aaaargh!

This one is true, and it was a pretty disgusting weapon.

A roadblock erected by the Home Guard

Women preparing for an invasion with walking sticks and umbrellas

When you couldn't get hold of a real weapon, a pretend one would do. People were encouraged to put suspicious-looking containers in the road with bits of wire dangling from them, so passing Germans would think they were bombs and would slow down.

You were even encouraged to prop open a window of your house and stick a bit of pipe out of it, so it would look as though there was a man inside with a gun!

# THE INVASION IS CANCELLED

Would the Home Guard have been able to hold off a German invasion?

No chance!!

Well, maybe not, but we'll never know, because in September 1940 Hitler changed his mind and decided not to invade Britain after all.

Why?

Well, the RAF was proving a very difficult enemy to beat. And anyway, why would he waste men and tanks, when he could just as easily bomb British towns and cities directly from the air until the people begged him for mercy? Britain was about to be on the receiving end of a hideous barrage of horrors from the sky!

# CHAPTER THREE
# NITS
# IN THE BLITZ

**H**itler's plan was to bomb London and Britain's other big cities to bits. He thought this would cause so much suffering it would force the British to surrender. The German bombers began their onslaught in September 1940 ...

They dropped more bombs in October 1940 ...

Even more in November ...

And December . . .

Again in January 1941 . . .

In February . . .

March . . .

April and May . . .

The bombing became known as 'the Blitz', after the German word for 'lightning', and it was pretty scary.

# LOTS OF BUSES

The first attack was on 7 September 1940 at about five o'clock in the afternoon. 350 German bombers flew in waves and dropped over 300 tons of high explosive on the capital.

300 tons, Wow!

Yes, that's about the same weight as twenty-five double-decker buses! Over the course of the Blitz the Germans dropped more than 18,800 tons of high explosive on Britain.

That's about . . . er . . . 1,500 double-decker buses' worth!

For over ten hours the bombing went on and on. Explosions rocked the streets, buildings burned, and on the River Thames, boats blazed. As night fell, the sky glowed orange. 436 people were killed and 1,600 were seriously injured.

If you're wondering what you have to do to be 'seriously injured' . . .

. . . as opposed to mildly injured, or just putting it on for a bit of sympathy and a cup of tea . . .

. . . you've got to have fractured or broken something, be bleeding inside, be burned, crushed, smashed to bits or knocked unconscious. In other words, it's preferable to being killed . . . but only just.

The following morning the bombing finally stopped. Everyone came out of hiding to look at all the damage. There were giant holes in the ground where buildings had been, bits of arms and legs lying in the street, and smoke and dust everywhere ...

It was horrible, but there wasn't much time to clean up – the bombers came back the next night ... and the next. They bombed London for fifty-eight nights on the trot! While the Blitz went on, nobody got much sleep.

Central London was smashed to pieces during the Blitz, but St Paul's Cathedral was spared

But it wasn't just London that was on the receiving end of all these deadly explosions. Lots of other big British cities were hit. It was particularly dangerous for people who lived near railways, factories and ports, because the Germans considered them important targets and wanted to destroy them. In fact no one was totally safe, because if the planes couldn't find anything important to bomb, they just dropped their deadly load anywhere.

# EATING TOOTHPASTE

The British government had realized that the Germans might try to bomb Britain's cities, so they'd stockpiled coffins and sandbags, handed out instruction leaflets and set up warning systems. They also wanted to try and make sure that Britain's kids were safe. Soon after the war began, a plan was launched to move 800,000 children out of the cities and into the countryside where they were less likely to be bombed. It was called 'Operation Pied Piper'!

'Operation Pied Piper'?

Yeah, remember that bloke in the flash tights with the flute, who got all the kids to follow him? That's what the government was doing. Geddit?

What, dressing up and playing a flute?

In towns everywhere, kids turned up at school and were given labels with a name, address and number on them. Once they'd put them on, they looked a bit like awkward-shaped parcels.

FAR FROM HOME

They were put on to buses and trains and shipped out (or 'evacuated') to towns and villages in the countryside. They were known as 'evacuees'.

They never knew exactly where they were going; they were just told to take enough food for two days. One girl evacuee got so hungry on the journey she ate her toothpaste!

When they finally arrived at their destination, they had to line up while local people came and took a look, chose which kid they wanted, and took them home.

Some kids loved it. They stayed with nice families, enjoyed the fresh air and made lots of new friends. But others had a horrible time. They missed their homes and were picked on by the locals for being smelly, dirty townies. Some evacuees came from poor city slums and had never seen a cow or eaten a vegetable in their entire life. Their host families complained that they were covered in lice, didn't know how to use a toilet and were scared of baths. One host mother asked if she could swap her evacuees for some different ones, because hers were 'rough and rude'.

London kids evacuated to Wales

Some hosts were too doddery to look after their evacuee children properly, while others were really nasty and beat them or locked them in cupboards. Perhaps it's not surprising that two-thirds of evacuee kids went back home within a few months!

## SCHOOL'S OUT!

Whether you were in the countryside or the city, the good news was that you probably weren't in school.

As soon as war broke out, schools everywhere closed. Adults were too busy with war-stuff to worry about whether kids could add two plus four or spell the word 'giraffe'.

Within weeks there were complaints that children were running wild in the streets, so makeshift schools were set up in homes and churches, and open-air lessons were held in local parks.

Eventually most schools re-opened, although if there had been an air-raid the night before, school kids got the next morning off to catch up on their sleep!

An open-air school

# SMELLING OF PEARDROPS

One of the things you practised at school (when it was open) was how to put on your gas mask.

The government gave out millions of weird-looking facemasks in case the Germans dropped bombs that gave off poisonous gas. Everyone had to carry one and had to learn how to put it on in a hurry.

# HOW TO PUT ON A GAS MASK

**1** Remove it from its box.

**2** Put it on your face.

**3** Breathe.

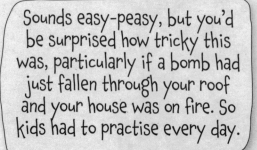

Sounds easy-peasy, but you'd be surprised how tricky this was, particularly if a bomb had just fallen through your roof and your house was on fire. So kids had to practise every day.

# HOW TO DETECT POISON GAS

☐ Tear Gas smells like peardrops.

☐ Blister Gas smells like geraniums.

☐ Poison Gas smells of mown grass.

If you smell any of these things, it's time to get your mask on quick.

# BLITZ QUIZ

What is the sensible thing to do when bombs start falling from the sky? Is it . . .

**1** Stand in the street, stare up at the sky, point and say *'Oooohhh, see that really big bomb? It looks like it's coming this . . . AAAARRRGHHH!!'*?

**2** Run round in circles, scream and wet yourself?

**3** Find a place to shelter, preferably somewhere under the ground with a very thick concrete ceiling?

If you didn't choose **3**, you'd better hope some loving family member comes round to scrape your smoking remains into a shoebox.

Lots of people built air-raid shelters in their gardens (which looked a bit like little metal sheds covered in earth).

Oi!

Others crowded into basements and cellars. Some went into the London Underground and slept on the platforms of the tube stations. This became so popular that there were queues outside the stations every evening. Eventually, the electricity was turned off at night, and from then on people could even sleep on the rails!

By the end of the Blitz more than 100,000 Londoners were sleeping in the Underground – so many that the government started providing them with bunk beds and toilets.

# OUCH!

Enemy bomber pilots found their way around by looking at the ground below. At night from the air most countries are a network of tiny glittering lights – little bright ones where the roads are, and clusters of them twinkling away in the towns and cities.

To make it harder for the pilots to find their targets, the government ordered a 'black-out' at night. This meant that absolutely no light was allowed. Windows had to be covered with thick black fabric or black paint, streetlights were turned off and you had to pay a fine if you were caught striking a match or shining a torch.

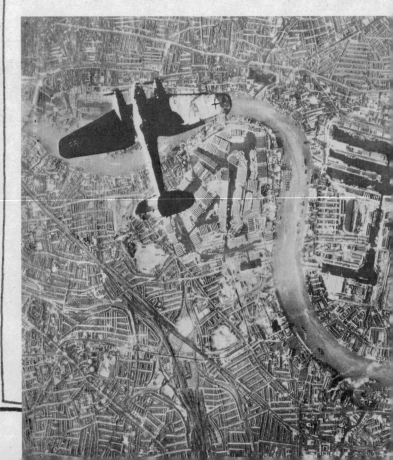

It was a good idea, but there were a few problems. People drove into trees, walked into lamp posts or fell into rivers while trying to find their way round after dark. Burglars and pickpockets no longer had to worry about being seen, and the crime rate soared.

To try and make life safer, kerbs and tree trunks were painted white and people were encouraged to wear white clothes that showed up in the dark . . . nevertheless people still kept bumping into things.

The government eventually gave in and said people could carry torches – as long as they were covered in two sheets of tissue paper and were held downward!

# STOP THE BOMBERS

Two kinds of weapon were invented to try and stop the bombers:

**THE BARRAGE BALLOON:** These were giant silver whale-sized helium balloons that floated in the sky, attached to the ground by steel cables. Any plane that got caught in the cables would get its wings ripped off. The German pilots had to fly really high to avoid them, which made their bombs less accurate.

**THE ACK-ACK GUN (or Anti-aircraft Gun):** These were designed to shoot German bombers out of the sky. They were ginormous, with 15-ft barrels (more than twice the height of a man). You needed a crew of eleven people to work each gun – two to wind the handles to position it, one to fire it, and eight to help load the massive shells.

Despite the guns and balloons, some bombers always got through, large parts of cities were destroyed, and more than 40,000 people were killed. Bombs also damaged famous landmarks like Buckingham Palace and Westminster Abbey.

# THE SUICIDE SQUAD

Not all bombs exploded immediately. One of the worst jobs in the war was getting rid of the ones which hadn't gone off. The people who did this were called the 'Bomb Disposal Squad' (otherwise known as the 'Suicide Squad'). One bomb-disposal expert, Lieutenant Talbot, was awarded a medal for bravery because he picked up a live time-bomb and carried it on his shoulder 200 yards to a safe place before it exploded!

## WELL DONE, BOY

They gave medals to animals as well. The first went to a dog called 'Chum', who helped dig his owner out of a collapsed air-raid shelter.

My hero!

# EAT YOUR HAT!

Despite all the bombs, destruction and death, most people tried to carry on as normal. They kept on working and going out at night (there was even a new dance called the 'black-out stroll'). Wrecked shops put out signs saying 'Business as Usual'.

One woman who was standing on the doorstep of her bombed-out house was asked how she felt. She said, 'Hitler can eat his hat for all I care. London folk will never give in.'

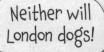

Neither will London dogs!

# CHAPTER FOUR
# FIGHT!
# FIGHT! FIGHT!
# FIGHT!

Yㅇㅇu may be thinking that the war was just between Germany and Britain. But if you are, you're wrong.

Germany and Britain both had 'Allies' – other countries all over the world who joined in to help them try and win.

## NOT YOUR BEZZY MATES

People who join up with you in order to fight someone else are called your 'Allies'. They may not be your bezzy mates, but if you stick together, you've got a better chance of winning.

Suppose the school bully picked on you. You might want to form an 'alliance' with as many classmates as possible in the hope that they'd stand by you and stop you getting clobbered. Of course, they might run away at the crucial moment. But that's the problem with 'allies': they aren't real friends and sometimes they change sides.

When World War Two broke out, lots of countries became Allies with either Britain or Germany, although a few of them (like Russia) changed sides halfway through!

Germany's Allies included . . .

**Italy**,

**Japan**,

Ciao!

Sziasztok!

**Hungary**,

**Romania** and

**Bulgaria**.

Zdrave!

We call the people who fought with Britain 'The Allies', while the ones who fought on Germany's side called themselves 'The Axis Powers'.

An 'axis' is the name for anything which other things revolve round. Basically the Germans and their allies thought that the world revolved around them! They were real big-heads!

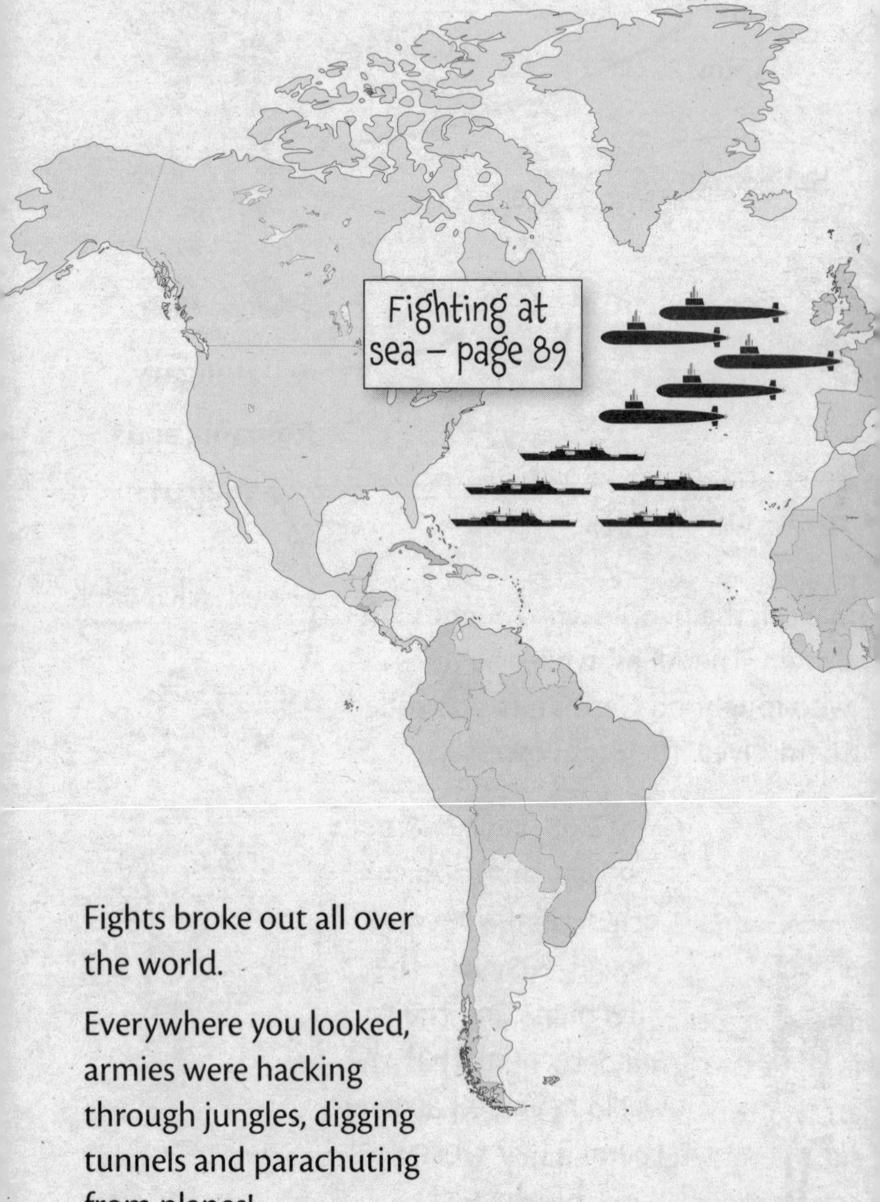

Fighting at
sea – page 89

Fights broke out all over
the world.

Everywhere you looked,
armies were hacking
through jungles, digging
tunnels and parachuting
from planes!

Fighting in the
snow – page 88

Fighting in the
desert – page 78

Fighting in the
jungle – page 100

There were soldiers in sandstorms fighting
in the deserts, soldiers in scuba diving suits
attacking boats along the coasts, sailors in
submarines fighting under the ocean and even
commandos on skis fighting in the mountains.

# ANOTHER WEIRDO

Italy was run by a nutter called Benito Mussolini.

Like Hitler, he was a power-crazed maniac who liked putting on an army uniform and beating up anyone who disagreed with him. He knew that whoever won the war would become rich and powerful, so when it looked like the Germans were winning, he joined in on their side.

He sent a load of Italian troops to invade Egypt, a country in North Africa. It was hundreds of miles from where most of the fighting was taking place, but his plan wasn't as mad as it sounds. There was a very long and important canal there called the Suez Canal, which was controlled by the British who used it to send their ships all round the world.

Mussolini knew that if he could take control of the canal, he could stop the Brits moving their army. British soldiers tried to stop him, and so did fighting men from Australia, South Africa, the Far East and New Zealand.

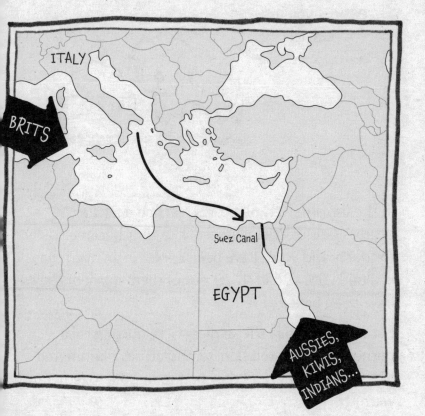

# SOLDIERS IN THE DESERT

Unfortunately, Egypt just happens to be surrounded by the Sahara desert, one of the hottest and driest places on earth, and fighting in a desert is hard work.

On the other hand, fighting in a dessert is easy – you just eat it!

In the daytime, temperatures reached a sizzling 50 degrees Celsius. Metal objects like guns became too hot to touch, and you'd have been cooler in an oven than in a tank. Crews had to get out of them quick or they'd have been baked alive!

But at night, while the soldiers were nursing their burned and blistered skin, temperatures plummeted to below freezing, and they had to huddle together for warmth.

79

And as for the sand, it got everywhere!

Sandstorms could last for days, and you couldn't see anything or anyone. Sometimes soldiers wandered off to the loo, got lost and were never seen again.

The Sahara desert is huge, and there were no towns or supplies for hundreds of miles, so armies had to carry their food and water with them over incredibly long distances. Soldiers sometimes even washed in petrol to save water . . . and all that was before the enemy started shooting at you!

# VERY HARD BLOKES!

The Allies had a special force of soldiers whose job was to travel behind enemy lines in the desert and spy on what the Germans were doing. They were really tough and had to live in the Sahara for weeks with just poisonous snakes for company. They navigated by the stars and learned how to read tracks in the sand so they could tell how many men, tanks and camels had crossed in which direction.

In 1941, nine of them were left stranded in the desert without transport. All they had to survive on were three gallons of water, a packet of nine biscuits, a piece of chocolate and a compass that had been rescued from a burning vehicle. In order to make their escape they had to walk 200 miles. Their sandals fell to pieces, so they wrapped their feet in cloth torn from their jackets. After eight days braving the heat, the cold and the dust storms they finally made it to the nearest oasis!

# THE DEVIL'S GARDEN

One of the big dangers in the desert was accidentally stepping on a landmine and getting your leg, hand, arm, head or all four blown off. Landmines were bombs hidden under the sand, which exploded when you stepped on them or drove over one in a tank.

Before the Battle of El Alamein in 1942 the Germans and Italians buried an incredible 500,000 mines across a five-mile strip of land to stop the Allies reaching them. They called this massive minefield the 'Devil's Garden'.

Allied engineers were sent to clear paths through the minefield and they didn't have lots of hi-tech kit to help them.

Both sides used mines. This is an Italian bomb-disposal team

# HOW TO CLEAR A PATH THROUGH A MINEFIELD WITHOUT HI-TECH KIT

Slowly!

Gently!

**1** Walk along, using your bayonet to prod the ground until you hear the clink of metal.

Carefully!

**2** Clear the dirt and sand away.

Gently I said!

**3** Make sure the mine's not connected by wires to any other mines nearby, then gently lift it out.

Aargh, it's too scary, I can't look!!

**4** De-fuse it by unscrewing it and removing the detonator from inside, all without accidentally setting it off!

At El Alamein, the engineers had to do this hundreds of times while gunfire echoed all around them. Eventually they managed to clear paths through the minefield which allowed the Allies to attack. The victory at El Alamein helped the Allies to win the Desert War. The Italians and Germans left North Africa in May 1943.

## PEEWEE'S GUIDE TO SOLDIERS' STUFF

Each army gave its soldiers slightly different bits and pieces to carry, but most of them were kitted out with . . .

**A GAS MASK** In case of a gas attack. They were heavy, were hardly ever needed and lots of soldiers left them behind or pretended they'd lost them.

**RATIONS** Soldiers in the field mostly lived on tinned beef, biscuits and the odd bit of chocolate. American soldiers were given packets of M&Ms.

**A HOUSEWIFE** No, not a tiny woman you put in your pocket. It was the soldiers' name for a sewing kit. It was for mending rips in your clothing and generally stopping all your clothes falling off.

**A RIFLE** This was a gun with a long barrel, so accurate it could hit an enemy up to 300m away.

**A BAYONET** If you missed, you could screw this handy dagger-like attachment on the end of your rifle, run up to your enemy and stab him!

**SPARE SOCKS** You'd sell your granny for a nice dry pair of these.

**A HELMET** It weighed about 3lbs, protected your head and could also be used as a seat, a washbasin or a cooking pot!

**A RADIO** To keep in touch with the rest of the army, specially trained soldiers had to carry big radios on their backs. They were about the same weight as a microwave oven.

**A WATER BOTTLE** You'd probably have to fight in places where fresh water was in short supply. Soldiers often brushed their teeth, shaved and made a cup of tea all with the same cupful of water! Bleurgh!

**A SPADE** To dig holes to hide in, and also to go to the loo in.

# THE MAN OF STEEL

The Italians weren't the only ones who'd joined the war on Germany's side. Russia did too.

Its leader was a man called Josef Besarionis dze Jughashvili.

That's a bit of a mouthful!

Yes, but he changed it to Joe Stalin when he was in prison because it made him sound hard.

What's so hard about your name, Mr Stalin?

It means 'Man of Steel', little girl!

Young Joe was a criminal mastermind with a violent streak. He'd been sent to prison eight times!

But I escaped seven times, ho ho ho!

He'd been involved in street brawls, bank robberies, kidnapping, arson attacks and murder.

He wasn't just a dumb thug, though: he had big ambitions – he wanted to rule Russia. He joined a political party called the 'Bolsheviks' and used his criminal skills and stolen money to help get them into power. When the leader of the party died, Stalin took over. Once he was in charge, he ruled the country with an iron fist, imprisoning or murdering anyone he didn't like (one guy he **really** didn't like was found dead with an ice-pick in his head).

Whoops!

When the Second World War started, Stalin joined in on Germany's side. He wanted more land in Eastern Europe and thought now was a good time to grab it.

## SOLDIERS ON SKIS

While some soldiers were fighting in the deserts of Africa, others were battling in deep snow . . . and it was all because of Stalin.

Soon after the war broke out, the Russian leader ordered hundreds of thousands of Russian soldiers and tanks to invade the neighbouring country of Finland.

The Finns were outnumbered and outgunned, but they had one big advantage – they were used to the weather. Finland lies on the edge of the Arctic circle – which means it gets cold . . . *really* cold . . . colder than a snowman in a freezer.

The Finns fought on skis and wore white padded uniforms, which kept them warm and made them invisible in the snowy landscape. They used to sneak up on the Russian troops, attack them and disappear back into the forest.

One Finnish soldier known as the 'White Death' terrified the Russians – he shot over 500 of them.

It wasn't just soldiers and airmen who fought in World War Two. All round the world, sailors were risking their lives too.

## SOLDIERS UNDERWATER

Battles weren't only being fought on land. In the Atlantic Ocean another war was being waged between ships and submarines.

Britain and her Allies needed ships to transport food, guns and soldiers all over the globe.

But the Germans sent submarines called 'U-Boats' (short for Undersea Boats) to sink them. Groups of U-Boats would hunt in packs looking for ships to attack.

When they found one, they'd fire torpedoes into the ship's hull to try and sink it.

U-boats sank over 2,600 Allied ships during World War Two!

## SWINE BOATS

Lots of U-Boat crews spent as long as six months at sea without stopping at one single port. During all that time they weren't allowed to bathe, shave or change their clothes.

The food on board a U-Boat got covered in mould — loaves of bread were nicknamed 'rabbits' because they were so white and furry!

Pooh!

It was hot, damp and cramped, and with a crew of fifty men on board, the U-Boats soon got pretty stinky! In fact they were given the nickname 'swine boats' because of the smell! When they got to shore, all the bed clothes were burned – they were too filthy to be kept.

The British got fed up with German U-Boats attacking their ships all the time, so they made sure that they travelled in groups – called 'convoys' – protected by armed warships with plenty of firepower.

Ships also used listening devices to detect submarines underwater, so if there was a ship on the surface the entire U-Boat crew had to be totally silent, sometimes for hours at a time. They could only talk in whispers, and if they flushed the loo by mistake they'd probably be bombed to pieces!

# CHAPTER FIVE

## THE YANKS ARE COMING

**B**y the summer of 1941, lots of countries had joined in on Hitler's side: he'd conquered most of Europe, blitzed Britain, and his U-Boats had sunk a load of ships.

My plan's going pretty well, don't you think?

It was time to put the next bit of it into action. Since the beginning of the war he'd been secretly plotting to conquer Russia, wipe out the people living there and replace them with Germans. So he now ordered his army to invade it, even though the Russians were on his side.

In June 1941 a gigantic force of nearly 4 million soldiers, 3,350 tanks, 60,000 motor vehicles and 625,000 horses moved into Russia. The Russians were taken completely by surprise. In the quickest advance in human history, the German army travelled nearly 200 miles into Russian territory in just one week.

So did that mean the end of the Russians? No, luckily for them, three things slowed the German advance:

**1** **Its Size.** Russia was the largest country in the world, stretching halfway across the planet. It was absolutely, stonkingly, eye-wateringly ginormous. Even the Germans struggled to conquer it.

**2** **The Weather.** First it rained and then it snowed. The wet weather turned the dirt roads into muddy bogs and then into frozen muddy bogs. The Germans weren't prepared for the cold – they stuffed newspaper in their jackets to try to warm themselves up, but it didn't do much good. They caught pneumonia, their fingers and toes dropped off from frostbite, and many soldiers froze to death.

**3** **The Red Army.** The Russian Army was known as the 'Red Army' – it was massive (almost 2 million fighting men, thousands of tanks and tons of weapons) – and it fought like crazy to stop the Germans in their tracks. Mind you, it had to; Stalin made sure that if any of his men ran away, they were shot and their families were thrown in prison.

A German lorry stuck in the Russian mud, 1942

By the winter of 1941, the Germans were bogged down in the middle of Russia. This was bad news for Hitler and good news for Britain. Not only had Russia changed sides, but most of the German army were now freezing their bums off in Russia, rather than attacking the Brits.

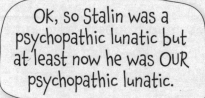

OK, so Stalin was a psychopathic lunatic but at least now he was OUR psychopathic lunatic.

Meanwhile there was a second bit of good news for the Allies. Guess who else was about to join in on their side?

## JAPAN MAKES A BIG MISTAKE

Halfway across the world, Japan became Germany's ally. Like Hitler and Stalin, the Japanese wanted an Empire. They decided to take over all the thousands of islands in the Pacific Ocean. Their plan was that the Germans would rule the West, while they would have their own island-empire in the East.

In December 1941, they sent in troops to seize some of the bigger Pacific islands. They knew that if they acted quickly, the Allies would be caught by surprise and wouldn't be able to stop them.

At the same time they sent planes and submarines to destroy a fleet of American ships in Pearl Harbor on the island of Hawaii. They thought everyone would be so

shocked and impressed at the speed of their invasion and the suddenness of their attacks, that they'd back off and let Japan keep its new territory.

They were wrong. These tactics just made everyone really, *really* angry; and the angriest of all were the Americans.

Boy! We're really, really mad!

Until then they'd stayed out of the war.

They'd helped the Allies a bit by giving them money, weapons and aircraft, but they didn't want to send over actual soldiers in case they got shot. But *now* Japan had attacked American ships. As one Japanese general said, 'I fear we have awakened a sleeping tiger ...'

## THE MAN IN A WHEELCHAIR

Franklin Delano Roosevelt caught a horrible virus called polio, and had to spend the rest of his life in a wheelchair. But did that stop him? ... Did it heck!

No, not only did he become the President of the United States, but he turned out to be one of the best Presidents the Americans had ever had.

When Japan attacked those ships at Pearl Harbor, Roosevelt decided it was time for America to go to war, bigtime!

Roosevelt was hardly ever photographed in his wheelchair. A lot of Americans didn't even know he used one

# SURPRISE, SURPRISE!

The Japanese surprised everybody ... and nobody was more surprised than the British.

They couldn't have been more surprised if the Japanese had jumped out of a giant cake wearing a gorilla costume and holding a big banner saying 'SURPRISE!'

**Surprise Number 1:** Britain had a big colony in South East Asia called 'British Malaya'. It included a giant military base on the island of Singapore which the British thought the Japanese would never dare attack.

But they were wrong. On 8 December 1941 the Japanese invaded that too.

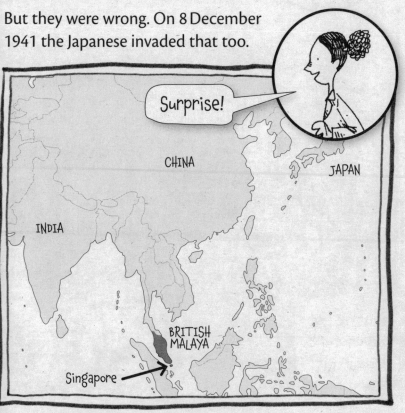

Surprise!

CHINA

JAPAN

INDIA

BRITISH MALAYA

Singapore

**Surprise Number 2:** Even if the Japanese did attack, the British had been confident they would attack by sea. So they'd built lots of walls, forts and guns around Singapore pointing out towards the water.

But the Japanese didn't attack from the sea: they came through the jungles and swamps to the north. Lots of them used bicycles and cycled along the jungle paths.

Surprise!

Anyone got a puncture repair kit?

**Surprise Number 3:** The British also had loads of planes and ships that could be used to scare off attackers.

But at the same time as bombing Pearl Harbor, the Japanese also bombed the British airbases on Singapore, so all their planes were destroyed. And when the British sent ships to stop the Japanese, they were sunk by torpedoes.

Surprise!

**Surprise Number 4:** Even if it did come to an actual battle, the British had a massive army, which would soon stop the Japanese in their tracks. Everybody knew the Japanese were rubbish at fighting and would give in easily.

But the Japanese turned out to be battle-hardened and bloodthirsty fighters who attacked with speed and ferocity. The British army was soon retreating and by February 1942 the Japanese had taken Singapore, and over 60,000 British, Indian and Australian soldiers were killed or captured.

Surprise!

British soldiers in Singapore surrender to the Japanese

Churchill called the fall of Singapore the worst disaster in British military history.

It was going to take the help of the Americans to stop the Japanese advance. By March 1942, American ships and troops were flooding into the Pacific.

## GOING MAD IN THE JUNGLE

Thousands of American soldiers were sent to recapture the Pacific islands. The weather was hot and humid and the islands were often covered in thick jungle and swamps. In the rainy season, everything got soaked and the soldiers' uniforms and kit rotted. Wounds didn't heal and they got pus-filled ulcers on their skin which attracted flies. Crocodiles lurked in the rivers and ate the dead bodies after each battle. Clouds of mosquitoes spread malaria which caused fevers, vomiting and hallucinations.

To make matters worse, the Japanese soldiers were as scary as scary can be!

## GUTS ON THE GROUND

For centuries the people of Japan had been isolated from the rest of the world, ruled over by of warriors known as the 'Samurai'.

You didn't want to annoy the Samurai. They were the only people who were allowed to own swords and fight anyone who didn't show them enough respect. They lived by a strict code known as the 'Way of the Warrior'. If a Samurai was ever defeated in battle, he had to kill himself by using his own sword to cut his stomach open so his guts would fall out!

By the time World War Two began, the Samurai didn't rule Japan any more, but lots of Japanese soldiers still believed in the Samurai code of fighting to the death and killing themselves rather than surrendering.

# IWO JIMA

The Americans attacked each island in the Pacific one-by-one and recaptured them – a slow and agonizing process.

One of the last islands they took back was called Iwo Jima. It was defended by 22,000 Japanese soldiers who had built pillboxes all over it connected by a network of deep trenches, tunnels and 'spider holes' (holes in the ground with just enough room for one person to jump out and shoot you).

## THE LEAST FUN PLACE TO BE IN WORLD WAR TWO

The Japanese thought any soldier who surrendered (without first gutting themselves in shame) deserved no respect. Japanese officers often treated captured soldiers like a piece of particularly smelly dog poo on the bottom of their shoe. Many troops from the British Empire were treated with vile cruelty, but Americans had a terrible time too.

One American soldier, Albert Parker, remembered being captured by the Japanese at a place called Bataan in 1942. He was made to march to a prison camp 65 miles away along, with thousands of other Prisoners of War. They didn't have any food and had to drink dirty ditch water to stay alive; any stragglers were beaten to death or bayoneted; the fallen were decapitated by Japanese officers swinging samurai swords.

In 1945, 60,000 US soldiers landed on the island, backed up by 800 warships. The Japanese were forced back, but fought every step of the way, shooting, stabbing with bayonets and hurling themselves at the attackers. One hill in particular was nicknamed the 'meat grinder' because so many soldiers died when the Americans tried to capture it. Even after the Japanese knew they'd lost control of the island, they charged towards the enemy screaming and trying to wipe out more enemy soldiers before getting shot themselves.

Iwo Jima cost the Americans the lives of almost 6,000 soldiers, with another 17,000 wounded – all to capture an island only five miles long.

This statue in Washington DC commemorates the raising of the American flag on Iwo Jima

# KAMIKAZE!

It wasn't just Japanese soldiers who resorted to crazy tactics. Japanese pilots volunteered to carry out suicide missions, flying their planes straight into Allied ships and blowing them up. These flights were known as 'Kamikaze missions' (Kamikaze means 'divine wind').

Tactics like this might sound mad but they scared the bejeebies out of the American troops. They thought the Japanese were barking mad – and no one likes fighting mad people: they might do anything!

## MEANWHILE IN ITALY . . .

Rome is here

American troops didn't just fight in the Pacific. Three days after declaring war on Japan, the USA declared war on Germany and Italy as well.

Now the Americans were on their side, the Allies decided to launch a fresh attack. In 1943 Allied forces invaded southern Italy using soldiers from Britain, America, Canada, India, New Zealand and Poland.

Allies land here

They thought this would be a doddle, and reckoned they'd be sitting in a nice restaurant in Rome within weeks, eating spaghetti bolognese with a sprinkle of parmesan cheese. At first, it looked like they'd be right. The Italians knew they didn't stand a chance and soon surrendered. But that wasn't the end of the story – not by a long shot!

Monte Cassino looked pretty before the war . . .

The Italians might have given up but the Germans had other ideas. They moved into Italy and fought to stop the Allies getting any further.

Nevertheless the Allied troops slowly pushed north through Italy, but it was tough going – the only route to Rome was through the mountains! It was wet and cold, the ground was rocky and the only shelter was a few spiky gorse bushes, with booby traps, barbed wire, and landmines hidden underneath!

Monte Cassino was a famously beautiful monastery in the mountains – or at least it *was*, until it became the focus of a long and bloody battle. It was bombed time and time again and attacked by waves of soldiers as they tried to dislodge the Germans from the site. It took six months and four big battles to take over the monastery. By the end, all that remained was a smoking heap of rubble!

The Allied troops finally reached Rome in June 1944.

# CHAPTER SIX

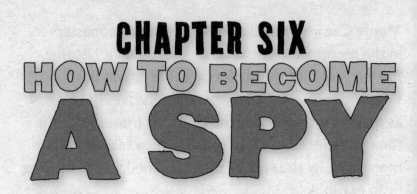

**P**ssst!
Reader!

Yes. Can you keep a secret?

Even a really juicy one?

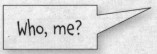

Can you lie convincingly under pressure?

Even when someone's giving you a Chinese burn or your mum's staring at you with a cross face?

Yes.

Can you be really really sneaky, like taking the last Chocolate Hobnob and pretending the dog ate it?

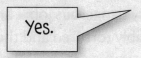
Yes.

Then congratulations, you'll make an excellent spy. You'd better start practising foreign languages and building up a collection of fake moustaches right away, so you'll be ready when you get tapped on the shoulder and are asked to become a member of . . .

**CHURCHILL'S SECRET ARMY!!**

SHHHHH!!

Winston Churchill realized that it was going to take more than luck to win the war, so he set up a secret organization called the 'Special Operations Executive' (or SOE), otherwise known as Churchill's Secret Army. If you worked for it, you became a spy and your job was to travel secretly into Nazi-controlled Europe. You had to pass on any useful information, and blow up enemy trains, factories and bridges. At the height of the war there were over 13,000 people doing this very dangerous job – anyone caught was arrested, horribly tortured and then shot by a firing squad.

## SPY SCHOOL

If you were brave and clever enough to join the secret squad, you were taught useful things like map-reading, unarmed combat and how to use dangerous weapons. But you also learned a whole host of other sneaky tricks, like how to pick locks, copy keys, write secret messages and blow things up before walking away whistling and pretending you didn't have anything to do with it.

Then you were parachuted into enemy territory, and in order to avoid being detected, you learned how to jump out of a plane at a low height without squishing into the ground.

You also had to wear a disguise, and were given a fake name and a 'cover story'. This meant making up things like where you were born, who your mum and dad were, and how many brothers and sisters you had, so that if anyone asked, your lies would be really convincing.

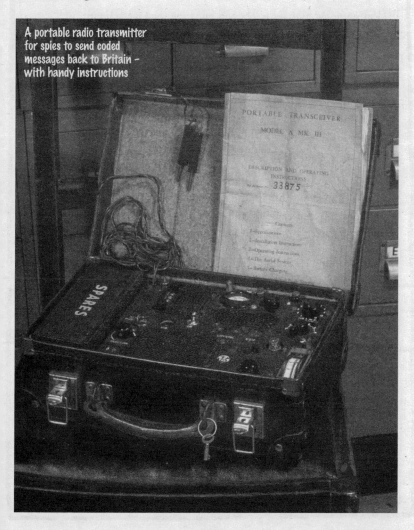

A portable radio transmitter for spies to send coded messages back to Britain – with handy instructions

## BEAUTIFUL AND DANGEROUS

Lots of Churchill's spies were women. They were chosen because they'd arouse less suspicion. Who would suspect Mrs Brown round the corner, in her woolly cardigan and baggy tights, of being an undercover spy?

But some women were chosen because they were beautiful and deadly. Kyrstyna Skarbek was a Polish aristocrat. On one occasion she parachuted into France, chatted up some German guards, and persuaded them to release a group of British spies they'd captured. Another time she secretly skied over mountains and through blizzards to get into Poland and recruit Polish agents.

She narrowly escaped capture by the Nazis several times. Once she pretended to be seriously ill by biting her tongue so hard that she coughed up blood. Another time she was stopped by two German guards at a border crossing and produced two live grenades. When the guards ran away she chucked the grenades at them and escaped across the border!

# CHURCHILL'S SPY TOY SHOP

Secret agents need secret weapons. In the Second World War many were developed and stored in a secret room in the Natural History Museum in London which became known as 'Churchill's Toy Shop'.

Wow!

They even stuffed dead rats with explosives. They hoped that the enemy would want to get rid of the furry little bodies, and would throw them in the fire, which would then explode.

If you think all this sounds like something out of James Bond, you're not far wrong. The author Ian Fleming, who wrote the James Bond books, worked with the Special Operations Executive, and based his characters on real secret agents!

# SECRET KIDS

The SOE weren't the only secret fighters. In every occupied country local people, like farmers, railway workers and housewives, fought the Nazis. They were known as 'The Resistance' because they resisted the enemy taking over their countries.

Sometimes Resistance fighters set up their own little armies in the mountains, but often, especially in the towns, they were as secret as Churchill's Secret Army, and sabotaged roads, railways and factories. Kids, who were unlikely to attract attention from the Germans, often became involved, running messages and helping Allied airmen get back to Britain.

A member of the French Resistance sets a bomb

## THE SPY IN A COFFIN

One member of the French Resistance was a middle-aged woman called Berthe Fraser. To her neighbours she was just a normal housewife, but in secret she helped British agents working in France. She gave them shelter, arranged transport and safe hiding places, organized meetings and carried messages hidden in her bags of shopping. Once she was asked to help an important British spy travel across France without being detected, so she organized a funeral procession and hid him in the coffin!

Eventually the Germans captured her, put her in prison and tortured her. She was stripped and flogged in public but she refused to give away the names of her friends in the Resistance. She was rescued in September 1944 when the Allies stormed the camp where she was held. She is supposed to have said to her rescuers, 'Thank you, boys, you're just in time.'

## BRAVE KIDS

Did you know that one of the first acts of resistance in the Second World War was carried out by a group of schoolkids? In November 1940, after the Nazis had taken over France, some French schoolchildren gathered in the centre of Paris and publicly celebrated the defeat of the Germans in World War One! This was a really dangerous thing to do. It was like sticking out your tongue at Hitler and blowing a raspberry at him – you can imagine how mad he could get if he thought people were taking the mickey out of him.

## ESCAPE ARTISTS

When Allied fighters were captured, they became Prisoners of War and were put into big camps watched over by German guards. Many tried to escape and with the help of the Resistance some were successful.

One Prisoner-of-War camp in Poland called Stalag Luft III was the scene of some very daring escapes. For instance, a group of prisoners pretended to be doing exercises in the prison yard, taking turns jumping over a large box-like wooden vaulting horse. What the German guards didn't know was that underneath the horse, two prisoners were busy digging a tunnel!

At the end of each day they'd cover the tunnel entrance with a piece of wood, and shovel earth on top of it, then they'd be carried back to their huts inside the horse. After lots of vaulting, the tunnel was finally ready and three men managed to escape and return to Britain!

# BRAINBOXES

One problem with trying to work out what the Germans were up to was that they sent all their messages in a complicated secret code. They'd invented a special machine, a bit like a typewriter, and when they typed a message in, the machine scrambled it all up.

It was called the 'Enigma Machine' – an 'enigma' is another word for a puzzle. The person you sent the message to had to have another machine and know the settings you used, so they could unscramble the message.

All the messages Britain and her Allies intercepted were total gobbledygook. This was incredibly frustrating. Imagine having a message in front of you that you KNOW is important but you can't read it! Grrrr . . .

So the British recruited lots of very clever mathematicians, engineers and scientists and told them to find out how the Enigma machine worked.

These brainboxes managed to get their hands on part of one of the German Enigma machines, then built an enormous computer the size of a room, which could calculate all the different settings and decipher the words. Now they could read all the enemy's messages and find out what they were planning – it was a massive advantage for the Allies!

See, it wasn't just the blokes fighting who won the war. Geeky people like me helped too!

# CHAPTER SEVEN
## CARROTS, CARROTS AND MORE CARROTS

Yum!

While British troops were fighting overseas, back home people was doing their bit for the war too.

I'm an ambulance driver!

Before it started, most women didn't have paid jobs. They left school, got married and spent their lives looking after their families, cleaning the house, cooking the tea, doing the washing and making sure everyone had clean pants for the next day. But when war broke out and most men were sent away to do the fighting, women were left to do all the other jobs that needed doing. In fact, without them the war effort would have ground to a halt.

They worked in factories, built planes, made guns, bombs and bullets, operated searchlights, fired anti-aircraft guns, drove fire engines, fixed cars, served as nurses in hospitals and worked in the fields growing and picking all the crops.

Then they went home, cooked the tea, cleaned the house, did the washing and made sure everyone had a clean pair of pants for the next day, just like before!!!

## WOMEN AT WAR

Some women even joined the armed forces.

This is a picture of my mum, Phyllis Robinson, who was a corporal in the Women's Royal Air Force, and my dad, Leslie Robinson, who was in the RAF.

## WHAT'S IN YOUR KNICKERS?

Before the war, Britain got most of its food from abroad. But as soon as the fighting started, German U-Boats began sinking the ships which brought supplies to the UK. Meanwhile some countries that had previously been our suppliers were now

Britain's enemies – so our food started running out.

Oi! Stop running out!

To make sure there was enough to go round, lots of foodstuffs were 'rationed', which meant you were only allowed a certain amount of them. Everyone got issued with a 'ration book' with coupons which told you how much you could have.

Even restaurants and hotels had to ration their food.
For instance, hotels were only allowed to serve a
one-sixth of an ounce of butter with each meal . . .

That's a tiny sliver about the thickness of a pound coin!

There's enough butter here for 18,745 people . . . probably

This graffiti man appeared whenever something was in short supply. He's called Chad!

WOT! NO BANANAS?

Foods like lemons and bananas, which only grew in faraway countries, disappeared from the shops. And with the usual types of meat in short supply, people started eating rabbit, horse and even whale!

To cope with all these food shortages, families were encouraged to grow their own vegetables and keep tasty animals like hens, rabbits, goats and pigs in their back yards. Parks, gardens and even school playing fields were turned into giant vegetable patches! Some people bought food illegally, or even stole it. One woman who worked as a waitress smuggled pieces of salmon, steaks and kippers out of her restaurant in her knickers!

Fancy a nice chop?

## WOT! NO CARROT CAKE?

One of the few things that wasn't in short supply was carrots, so everyone ended up eating lots of them. The government even designed a character called Dr Carrot who encouraged people to try carrot curry, carrot jam, toffee carrots and a drink called 'Carrolade' made out of, you guessed it, carrots.

DOCTOR CARROT *guards your Health*

But it wasn't just food that was in short supply. Petrol, clothing, coal, gas and electricity were rationed too, along with paper, furniture and soap. Even the number of pockets, buttons and pleats on your new clothes and the amount of lace you could put on a pair of frilly panties were restricted. Stockings were so hard to get hold of that women pretended they were wearing them, even though they weren't. They rubbed gravy browning on their legs, and drew the seams on with a pen!

# SEARCH FOR SCRAP

So much metal was needed to make weapons that thousands of people sacrificed their aluminium cooking pots so they could be melted down and turned into metal for aircraft. One eighty-year-old granny walked a whole mile to hand in her old saucepan. But it wasn't just pots and pans that were sacrificed. People gave aluminium cigarette cases, bedsteads, bicycles, railings . . . someone even donated an artificial leg, and someone else a racing car! In one town so much was collected, they had to use a steam-roller to flatten it all before it was carried away.

Some people say that all this collecting was a big publicity stunt, and that lots of the scrap was never melted down. Instead it was just dumped in the River Thames.

But mysteriously all the government records about the scrap collection were destroyed – so we'll never know for sure!

Berlin in 1945

## SHEER HELL

Things may have been difficult in Great Britain, but the people of some countries suffered much more.

For instance, in Russia, where the German and Russian armies were fighting for control of the city of Leningrad, life was sheer hell. The streets were a battleground and the Germans blocked off all supplies to the city and bombed the Russian food stores.

Food became so scarce that your entire daily food ration was 125 grams of bread (about four slices) which was mostly made up of sawdust! People ate anything they could, including their pets. More than half a million people died of hunger.

# EVEN WORSE THAN SHEER HELL

The next three pages tell a very horrible story . . .

But it's also a very important one.

You decide whether you want to read it or not.

For Jewish people living in German-occupied countries, things got even worse. The Nazis rounded them up and forced them into 'ghettos', which were special areas of towns and cities where they were separated from the rest of the population. They were packed so tight that six people lived in each room!

Jewish familes forced out of their homes in Poland

When rations were introduced, Jewish people got less than anyone else and weren't allowed any meat, eggs, bread or milk. The Nazis knew this meant lots of them would starve, but when they didn't die quickly enough, Hitler's men decided on something even more drastic. They packed all the Jewish people they could find into trains and sent them to special camps.

Discarded Jewish clothing in a concentration camp

Once there, the fit and healthy ones were used as slave labour until they died of exhaustion. The old and the very young, including babies, children and the sick, were considered to be useless. They were herded into special chambers and poison gas was pumped in to kill them.

Some people risked their lives by hiding Jewish people in their houses, or helping them escape to other countries. German businessman Oskar Schindler protected the hundreds of Jewish people who worked in his factory in Poland. He persuaded the Nazis that they were doing valuable work for the war effort and couldn't be sent to the camps, and when it became too dangerous for them to stay at home he let them live in his factory. He is thought to have saved the lives of over 1,000 people.

Millions of Jews were murdered by the Nazis.

We must all try to make sure nothing like this ever happens again.

That's why saying 'NO' to racism is so important . . .

. . . whether it's at school, or on the playing field or among your friends.

Dogs wouldn't do anything like that. Humans can be really horrible sometimes.

# CHAPTER EIGHT

# D-DAY!

By spring 1944 the Red Army was beating the Germans in the snowy wastes of Russia, the Americans had joined in on the Allied side, and Mussolini's Italian army had been defeated. It was time to take Europe back from Hitler.

So the Allies planned a massive invasion – a huge army of British, American and Canadians who would cross the Channel and land in Normandy on the coast of France.

## HOW TO FAKE AN INVASION

But they needed to build so many ships, planes and guns, that any German plane flying overhead would spot them and guess what was happening right away. How could they keep the invasion a surprise?

Their solution was to hatch the all-time sneakiest plan ever. They pretended the invasion was going to land somewhere else! That way Hitler would order his troops to defend the wrong place!

To fool him they created a pretend invasion force complete with inflatable rubber tanks and planes, dummy airfields and fake landing craft, and used sound systems on the back of trucks to broadcast the noise of an army on the move. They even broadcast fake radio messages between non-existent ships, while at the same time dropping bundles of tiny metallic strips from aircraft that gave the impression on enemy radar screens of a massive incoming bomber raid far inland. The Germans were totally fooled.

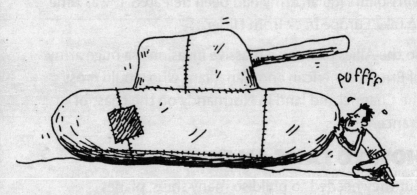

In fact, the trick worked so well that when the real invading army landed, Hitler thought it was a diversion from the actual invasion and held off sending his army to stop it.

So now it was time for 'D-Day', the code-name for the day the real Allied invasion of Europe was planned to begin. If it worked, it was pretty certain that the Germans would be defeated. But first the Allied Army had to get ashore!

Just after midnight on 6 June 1944, 24,000 paratroopers were dropped into enemy territory. Their job was to block roads and capture bridges to stop the Germans sending in their army when they found out about the invasion.

But in the darkness and heavy fog, not all the paratroopers landed where they were supposed to. Some dropped into swamps, others splashed into ponds or ended up on the roofs of buildings. One paratrooper was left dangling from a church spire! (Whoops!) Others landed with their parachutes riddled with holes after being shot at by German guns. (Gulp!)

Nevertheless many of them managed to find their targets, and blew up bridges, cut phone lines and ambushed the German positions.

Then at 6.30 the next morning, the main invasion began. A massive force of over 150,000 troops landed on the beaches of Normandy.

And it wasn't just soldiers who came ashore. Boats delivered masses of food, guns, tanks, lorries and ammunition so that the invading army would have enough supplies.

This was the largest sea-borne invasion in history!

# A DAY AT THE BEACH

The beach landings were no picnic. There was fierce fighting. Ships were fired at and exploded in huge balls of flame, men were shot or drowned as they tried to reach the beach.

Once on dry land, some soldiers were given orders to get to the top of 100-foot-high cliffs to try and destroy the German guns that were pointed at the beach. If they failed, so might the invasion. They fired rocket-propelled hooks up to the top of the cliffs, leaving ropes dangling down. As they made their wet and slippery way up the rock face, the Germans above shot at them and tried to cut their ropes! Eventually they made it to the top, and managed to find the German guns and destroy them before they could be used against the Allies below.

2,500 soldiers died on D-Day, but more than 150,000 made it safely to shore! The invasion had begun!

The D-Day invasion begins

The Allies begin to move into France

## MAGIC BULLETS

The Allied soldiers carried 'magic bullets' with them. No, I don't mean they'd been conjured up by wizards with white beards who cast spells and made bullets magically hit their targets. That would have been ridiculous . . . although also very cool.

'Magic bullet' was the name doctors used for a special type of medicine – one that was so effective, it seemed to work by magic.

The soldiers had actually been given little packets of a special new drug called 'penicillin'. Before it was invented, lots of people died from small infections, because when they cut their skin, dirt got into it, along with lots of tiny living things called 'bacteria' which can spread infection.

They never had that sort of thing in my day!

Penicillin works by killing these bacteria, and during World War Two, scientists in Britain and America worked hard to produce stockpiles of the stuff. Finally, by D-Day there was enough to treat all the injured Allied soldiers involved in the invasion, which saved thousands of lives!

## THE RACE FOR BERLIN

From the coast, the Allies then pushed inland. Meanwhile on the other side of Europe, Stalin's Red Army was pushing eastward. Hitler and the German army were trapped in the middle!

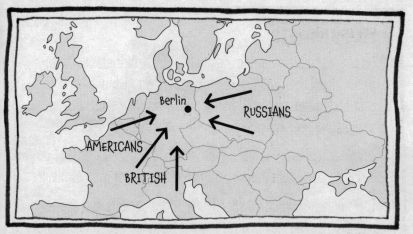

The British, American and Russian armies raced towards Germany's capital city, Berlin. At the same time, Allied planes dropped thousands of bombs on German cities to force them to surrender. In fact the Allies dropped more bombs on Berlin than the Germans dropped on the whole of Britain.

One German city called Dresden was so badly bombed that the whole city was flattened and the explosions caused a storm of fire which killed 25,000 German men, women and children.

## GOODBYE, HITLER

In Berlin, Hitler ordered his men to defend the city to the death, while he hid in an underground bunker. But there weren't enough soldiers available, so kids from the Hitler Youth were given guns and helmets and told to fight the approaching Allied armies! Children as young as eight had to face some of the most battle-hardened soldiers in the world. Their chances of surviving were very low.

The German government building after the Allied bombing

Some people thought the Allied bombing was fair because it gave the Germans a taste of their own medicine.

Others reckoned it made the Allies just as bad as the Nazis.

What do you think?

Soon the Russian Red Army had reached the outskirts of Berlin. Meanwhile, down in his bunker, Hitler received news that in Italy his fellow dictator, Benito Mussolini, had been caught trying to run away, had been shot by a firing squad, and that an angry crowd had hung his body upside down from a meat hook.

Hitler finally realized the war was lost. Within days the Russians would be knocking on the door of his bunker, saying something like . . .

Hello, Mr Hitler, it's meat-hook time!

So two days later he poisoned his beloved pet dog Blondie and then shot himself. Germany surrendered. The war in Europe was over! Big celebrations broke out all over the world from Moscow to New York!

Celebrating in Trafalgar Square

Hooray! Back to the ironing and washing-up!

There was only one *small* snag. Over in the Pacific, the war was still raging. The Japanese weren't going to give in easily!

## THE WORLD'S DEADLIEST WEAPON

After six years and a lot of bloodshed most people were pretty sick of the war, so the Allies made a decision to end it quickly, the only way they knew how.

They would launch a weapon so deadly, so destructive and so mind-numbingly, jaw-droppingly terrifying, that the Japanese would give up immediately!

And the Americans had got exactly that kind of weapon. It was called 'the Atomic bomb' and it was 2,000 times more powerful than a normal bomb. The scientists knew that when it exploded, it would create a massive fireball, and would send out shockwaves which would flatten buildings for miles around. Just one bomb would wipe out a city. But the Allies decided to drop not one, but two!

One was bad enough, two was horrendous. But the Allies didn't want the Japanese to think they only had one of these new bombs – they wanted them to think they had loads!

## HITLER'S BIG MISTAKE

Hitler's attack on the Jews wasn't just mean and stupid: it helped the Allies win the war.

When Hitler and the Nazis started picking on Jewish people, lots of clever Jewish scientists left Germany and went to live in Britain and America where they helped the Allies develop things like penicillin and the Atomic bomb!

# THE NOT SO LITTLE 'LITTLE BOY'

The first bomb was code-named 'Little Boy'. Which was a pretty strange name considering it was over 3 metres long and weighed more than a minibus!

It was dropped by plane over the Japanese city of Hiroshima on 6 August 1945. When it hit the ground, there was a blinding light, followed by a giant,

boiling-black, mushroom-shaped cloud that rose over 33,000 feet into the sky. 70,000 people were killed instantly. Some were crushed by falling buildings or suffocated in the smoke. Others were burned to a crisp, or were simply vaporized.

But the bomb didn't just kill people, it also made them sick. It produced invisible rays and particles that damaged people's bodies, and gave them what was called 'radiation sickness'.

For instance, two days after the explosion, a fourteen-year-old boy who was feeling poorly was admitted to hospital. Then his hair began falling out and his nose started bleeding. Within three weeks he was dead. There was nothing the doctors could do! Other people who survived the blast got cancer or had children who were born with disabilities.

All this may have been terrible, but it wasn't the end. The second bomb was dropped on a city called Nagasaki three days later. The Japanese surrendered within a week.

The war was over, but ordinary Japanese people paid a huge price.

An American sailor celebrating victory over Japan by snogging a passer-by

## DIDN'T ANYONE TELL YOU?

Actually, the war wasn't over for everyone.

Some Japanese soldiers fighting on remote islands in the Pacific never got the message! One soldier held out in the mountains of the Philippines for another 28 years. He hid in the jungle and shot at anyone who came near him, thinking they were the enemy. Several times people tried to tell him that the war had finished but he didn't believe them. In the end his old commander was found and was sent to the mountains to tell him that it really was all over!

## WHAT HAPPENED NEXT?

After the war ended, the surviving soldiers went back to their homes and families, cities were rebuilt and most people got on with their lives again.

But lots of top German and Japanese officials were arrested and were put on trial by the Allies. Many were convicted of terrible cruelty and of starting a war that had cost millions of lives, and were sentenced to death by hanging.

# UNITED NATIONS – NOT!

In 1945 the governments of the world got together and formed the 'United Nations'. This was a global peace-keeping force which tried to prevent massive wars from breaking out ever again.

But the peace only lasted about five minutes . . .

. . . and then countries started fighting each other like before, and wars have been happening ever since.

Luckily, none of them has been as big as the Second World War . . .

. . . and none of them has involved dropping another Atomic bomb.

Not yet anyway – paws crossed!

# TIMELINE

**1914–1918**   The Great War, later known as the First World War

**1929**   The Great Depression begins, and is about as much fun as it sounds

**1933**   Hitler takes charge in Germany

**1938**   German troops march into Austria

**May 1939**   Germany and Italy become allies

**1 Sep 1939**   Germany invades Poland – surprise!

**3 Sep 1939**   Britain and France declare war on Germany

**Nov 1939**   Russia invades Finland for some very chilly fighting

**May 1940**   Winston Churchill becomes Prime Minister of Britain

**28 May–4 Jun 1940**   Dunkirk – 338,000 British soldiers are saved from the beach

**Jun 1940**   The Germans take over Paris

**Jun 1940**   Italy joins the war

**Jul–Oct 1940**   The Battle of Britain is fought in the air

**7 Sep 1940**   The Blitz – the German campaign of air raids on Britain – begins

**Dec 1940**   British soldiers start fighting the Italians in North Africa

**Jun 1941**   Germany invades Russia – surprise again!

**Sep 1941–Jan 1944**   Life in Leningrad gets much more horrendous during the very long German siege of the city

**7 Dec 1941**  Japan destroys American ships at Pearl Harbor in Hawaii. The Americans get so angry that they join in the war

**15 Feb 1942**  Singapore falls to the Japanese. The British are miffed

**Oct–Nov 1942**  Battle of El Alamein – actually the second Battle of El Alamein, but this one's a very important win for the Allies

**Feb 1943**  The Germans surrender at Stalingrad in Russia – a major loss

**Feb 1943**  Britain and America begin regular bombing of Germany

**Jul 1943**  Allied soldiers land in Sicily, getting ready to invade mainland Italy. Shortly afterwards, the Italians overthrow Mussolini

**22 Jan 1944**  Allied soldiers land at Anzio in Italy

**4 Jun 1944**  The Allies make it to Rome

**6 Jun 1944**  'D-Day' – Allied soldiers invade France

**Feb 1945**  The Americans land on the island of Iwo Jima, and win it after a very tough fight

**Apr 1945**  Hitler kills himself in his bunker in Berlin

**8 May 1945**  Victory in Europe is celebrated, otherwise known as VE Day

**6 Aug 1945**  'Little Boy' is dropped on Hiroshima

**15 Aug 1945**  After Japan surrenders to the Allies, 'VJ Day' (Victory in Japan) is celebrated. The war is over

**Oct 1945**  The United Nations is founded, to try to make sure all this never happens again . . .

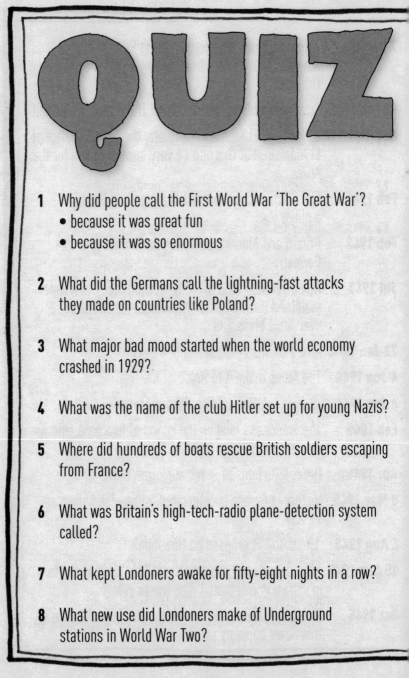

# QUIZ

1 Why did people call the First World War 'The Great War'?
 • because it was great fun
 • because it was so enormous

2 What did the Germans call the lightning-fast attacks they made on countries like Poland?

3 What major bad mood started when the world economy crashed in 1929?

4 What was the name of the club Hitler set up for young Nazis?

5 Where did hundreds of boats rescue British soldiers escaping from France?

6 What was Britain's high-tech-radio plane-detection system called?

7 What kept Londoners awake for fifty-eight nights in a row?

8 What new use did Londoners make of Underground stations in World War Two?

**9** If Britain and its friends were called 'the Allies', what was Germany's side in the war called?

**10** What sort of housewife could you keep in your pocket?

**11** Which leader's name meant 'Man of Steel'?

**12** What did deadly Finnish soldiers wear on their feet?

**13** Which country did the 'Red Army' fight for?

**14** What was the name given to Japanese suicide missions, meaning 'divine wind'?

**15** Where was 'Churchill's Toy Shop'?

**16** What was the Germans' top-secret code machine called?

**17** What was the codename for the Allies' invasion of Europe?
- D-Day
- i-Day or
- X-Day?

**ANSWERS** 1) Because it was so enormous.
2) Blitzkrieg. 3) The Great Depression. 4) The Hitler Youth.
5) Dunkirk. 6) Radar. 7) The Blitz. 8) Air-raid shelters. 9) The Axis.
10) A sewing kit. 11) Stalin. 12) Skis. 13) Russia. 14) Kamikaze.
15) In the Natural History Museum. 16) Enigma. 17) D-Day.

## Picture Credits

left to right
t = top; b = bottom; r = right; l = left; c = centre

Pages 9, 45, 100 Getty/Popperfoto; 10t, 18, 22, 26, 33, 55, 66, 67, 68, 116, 119, 127, 145 Getty/Hulton Archive; 10b Shutterstock/Tsurukame Design; 11, 101 Shutterstock/Everett Collection; 12, 53 Wikipedia; 15 Getty/AFP; 20 USHMM, courtesy of National Archives and Records Administration, College Park; 24, 94, 96, 106, 107, 131, 133 Getty/Time & Life; 31 Getty/AFP; 32, 35, 46 Getty/Archive Photos; 37t Shutterstock/Peter Baxter; 37b Shutterstock/Matt Gibson; 38t Shutterstock/johnbraid; 38b, 52, 57, 64, 80 Getty/IWM; 39 Shutterstock/141cocci; 40 Shutterstock/Yuyangc; 41 Shutterstock/Ivan Cholakov; 58, 124 Getty/Mansell Collection; 59 Getty/Science & Society PL; 63 Getty/Picture Post; 71 Shutterstock/Jeff Thrower; 81 Getty/Keystone France; 82 Getty/Mondadori; 87 Shutterstock/Olga Golovnev; 88, 90, 111, 147 Getty/Gamma-Keystone; 93, 98, 132 Getty/Roger Viollet; 103 Shutterstock/Brandon Bourdages; 104 Shutterstock/NeonLight; 112 Shutterstock/Trinacria Photo; 121 Shutterstock/mark higgins; 125 Tony Robinson own collection; 137, 139, 140 US Government Army Archives; 144 Wikipedia/No 5 Army Film Unit, US Military Archives; 148 Shutterstock/ Elena Schweitzer; 149 Getty/Michael Ochs Archive.

Tony Robinson's Weird World of Wonders is a multi-platform extravaganza (which doesn't mean it's a circus in a large railway station). You can get my World of Wonders game on line, there's a website, ebook, audio versions, extra stories and bits of weirdly wonderful design, marketing and publicity. In order to get all those things sorted out, I've surrounded myself with a grown-up version of the Curiosity Crew. They are Dan Newman (Design), Amy Lines (Marketing), Sally Oliphant (Publicity), James Luscombe (Digital), Tom Skipp (Ebooks) and Becky Lloyd (Audio). A big thanks to them all; they are committed, funny and extremely cool.

Tony has to say that otherwise they'd stop work and go home!

## Also available in this series

PLAY THE AWESOME WEIRD WORLD OF WONDERS GAME NOW AT

WWW.WEIRDWORLDOFWONDERS.COM